CW01500566

Noble Iniquity, Poems

Written by

Melanie M. Eyth

Dance of My Hands Publishing

IVYLAND, PA

Better it is for thee to have little,
than much of which may make thee proud.

Thomas à Kempis

Poems by Melanie Monterey Eyth.

All rights revert to the poet, and
all potential goodness to the world.

ISBN 0-9815887-2-7

Printed in the United States of America,
by Dance of My Hands Publishing.

Noble Iniquity, Poems

For Kathryn

What is Iniquity

If in anything thou seekest thyself,
great distress will come unto thee.
Love thyself last, thy neighbor second,
and thy God first.
I suppose I have not
followed my own advice,
for great distress comes unto me.

What We Must Do

The sweetness and kindness I offer
is generated and provided by the Holy Spirit,
and handed unto me by the Lord.
We must treat people with loveliness so
that they may better love the Lord and others.

Seeking Self-Discovery

Feelings of lostness overwhelm me and trouble me.
Mayn't I ever know the truth?
Will nothing ever improve for me?
Are we certain to find the things for which we seek?

This Earth Cannot Satisfy

If thou always runneth after satisfaction,
thou wilst certainly not find it.
As a dog chaseth its tail, so a person
chaseth futilely after earthly satisfaction.

Command to Release

I'd rather be alone and free than loved and chased.
Do not hold too tightly to me lest I die.
Anything grasped too firmly will surely want release.
Anything tied too tightly 'round my neck will choke me.

Alive in My Memory

God bless my former coworkers,
George, Nancy, Veronica, and Maggie,
sweet, hardworking, and
lovely as the Californian air.
I shall never forget thee.

Troubling Desire

Desire, desire,
you will ruin me!
Begone with you.

Discouraged

I'll never understand truth
because my mind is human-like
and flawed: pitiful, rash, and silly.

What Do I Deserve?

Growth, do I deserve?
Success?
Comfort?
Beauty?
Will any of these be mine?

Starved Heart

How can I love
another person fully
with this starved heart?

Fathers

The man who is almost my family
is very kind to me. The Bible says, *Lean
not on your own understanding, but in all your
ways acknowledge Him.* I shall depend on these
words. I shall love all my fathers.

Teller Lunch Break

My window is closed, closed,
closed. My window is closed,
I say, I'm free!

I Simply Love

Just because I love him, I
do not expect his love in return.
I do not expect his time or kindness.
I do not expect his affection or touch.
I simply love the shape of his head, the
flutttery movement of his hands when
he plays the guitar, when he sings in
that deep baritone voice. My heart
swells in his presence—and,
I simply love.

Anomaly

I possess lowborn sacrality
and highborn iniquity. Other pleasing
virtues include: impatience, envy, foolishness,
embarrassment, slothfulness, sadness, and hunger.
I possess many humilities of which I am very proud.
I possess many virtues of which I am very humble.

I Thought I'd Be Different

I've grown up,
and become something
other than expected. I had thought
I would become something else. This life
must belong to another: it cannot be my own.
The glamour, the riches, the comfort—I must
have stolen somebody else's life.

My Favorite Day of the Week

Tomorrow is Friday, then
Saturday, then Sunday the Sabbath.
They come every seven days, Sabbaths.
Over and over, like a dog to its bone,
I return to Church to hear the
good news.

Which Will Last Longer?

Innocence and experience are
woven together like fine silk, Blake
said. Surely, the world will outlast me.

Only He Sees Me

I am a grain of sand
in the ocean of time; my
relevance and power are less
than diminutive. I exist in
measurements known
<u>only</u> to the Lord.

Childless Woman

I ache for motherhood—
my hands itch to hold a baby;
my hips are bearing-hungry.

Time and Space

The shunning by others does not bother me. It assists
my mission, my quest, my intent. It ameliorates my drive
to create. I am thus free! The air is my friend, the nightly stars,
the distant clouds. I cry unto my Lord, companionship hinders me!
My art is desirous of nothing but uninterrupted time and space.

People Cannot Provide For Me

The Lord knows that I need more love than
the average person. I trust that He will lavish
his pure love upon me. I will open my heart
like a bowl and catch all of His love.

Customer Service Despair

It is not about me: the
treatment from customers,

the naiveté of customers. They
do not know—my despair
is meaningless.

Barred by Pride

They know not what they do to
me. They come to do their banking.
And I, a paid employee, must submit
completely to their whims and desires.
Behind the counter, I am like a human
machine, a mechanical heart and brain,
my pride the only barrier to peace and
satisfaction in this work.

From A Customer Service Representative

Dear Lord, let me be humble so that
I may serve the customers well. May my
impatience not show on my face. Remind me,
Oh Lord, over and over again, that I am Yours.
All necessary sweetness and kindness comes
from You. Help me to be good to them,
so that I may please you.

Justin

Justin, will I see your pretty aqua-colored
eyes again; flecked with gold and ringed with
black fire? Filled with sadness and wisdom:
knowing, affectionate, familiar. Your eyes
delight me more anyone else's. They
are a window to my own soul.

The Soul Dwelleth in the Body

The soul dwelleth in the body.
Commonly we mistake the body
for the soul or the soul for the body.
A line must be drawn—perhaps with
masking tape or chalk— so that we
may better differentiate the two.
One loves, and one does not.
One dies, and one does not.

The Flesh-Wants

The flesh-wants beckon like sugar,
sweet and lovely, wanting me to obey them.
But the soul is the true substance, and the flesh
is only temporary tissue: it has no lasting value
or rejuvenating strength. Feed the soul!

Employment

My appendages fling and flounder
like webbed feet trying to dance. I am
a loose bolt in their machine.

Good Night, World

Good night moon, good night
love, good night rest, good night
war, good night peace; crime, pun-
ishment, immorality, justice, worry,
harmony, organization, business,
capitalism, art, world!

My Baby

My baby, I will take care of you. I will huddle
you to my breast like a robin with its young. I will
build a nest for you inside my adult one. I will watch
over you with eyes of devotion and love. My wings
will protect you. I will share with you the story
of God, for He has given me you.

Song for Orphans

Help the little ones. Love the little ones.
Adore the little ones. Enlarge the hopes of
the little ones. Cradle the cares of the little
ones. Nourish the minds of the little ones.
Adopt a little one.

What Shall We Address if Not These?

Good morning men, women
and children. Good morning sun,
birds and flowers. Good morning
quietude and loveliness. Good
morning peace and joy.

May She and I Have Hope

The day is always young, and my
body feels so old. I have hope in my Lord,
but not in my body. Letting down, giving out,
and losing hope are of the weak-willed and non-
believing. May she and I have hope.

Delays Make the Hungering Soul the Ferventer

As John Bunyan says,
*Delays make the hungering
soul the ferventer.* To be weak
is to not believe. To be strong is
to believe. Hope will rest in the
spirit (truth) and not in the
flesh (falsity).

Warning

Of the flesh beware.
Of the soul truly care.

Waiting For My Love

I shall not commit myself to love
until the Lord says it is time for love.
My body, upon which is written, *delays
make the hungering soul the ferventer*, is
peachy and plump, soft and firm, ready
and warm, whilst I wait for my love.

Sparkle, My Friend

Sparkle, my friend,
as only thee can sparkle.
Thou has gifts and abilities
different than mine, but they
are as precious to me as my
own! Sparkle, loyal friend,
sparkle!

Nature Sings

Nature sings, ideas dance,
and people work. Let all the
world rejoice in the Lord!

My Career Is Unspecified

My career is unspecified,
my life unorganized, my body
unformed, my soul unfinished,
my family unattended, my
vision unseen.

My Soul Twin

My soul twin does not need me.
She lives and exists without me. My
soul twin inspires my work, and I hope
that I inspire hers, partly, as well. My
soul twin is a mother, now.

Lies We Tell Ourselves

I need ___ .
I desire ___ .
I hunger for ___ .
I must have ___ .
I cannot live without ___ .

Let Us Keep the Faith

Mr. Paris, the Lord will lavish
His love upon you. I know because
I have been praying that it will be so.

As The Deer

As the deer panteth for the water,
so my soul longeth for repose.

She Becomes A Flower

She becomes a flower when she dances.
She grows a garden when she dances. I am
thus reminded of the good in humanity.

The Sound of Dancing

Even the stones cry out when we dance.

Understanding Our Work

Perhaps moles understand the vitality of my
work—of every person's work, of the movement
of life. Perhaps moles understand things better than
we do, since they live deep in the heart of God's earth.

Will I Always Yearn For Freedom and Grace?

The time will come when another world will take me.
Ever do I yearn for freedom; ever do I yearn for grace.

Money Consumes My Thinking

Money consumes my thinking.
It is of normal occurrence— in this

world, to be consumed and addicted
to something so basic as money. So
I fit in well with the others.

Poetry Delights Me

Poetry delights me,
colors me, enlivens me,
creates me, defines me,
adorns me, shines me,
knows me.

Dancing

Dancing restores me,
calms me, cleanses me,
obeys me, justifies me,
helps me, frees me,
completes me.

God Bless You, Dad

God bless you, Dad. Your
legacy will be humble, like your
life. I have inherited your quietness.

My peaceful words and calm manner
are yours. I treat people with metered
gratitude and kindness, as you do.

I dress and style my hair plainly, as
you do. I eat what is placed before me.
I do not travel the earth seeking beauty,
because it has already been given to me.

I am satisfied. God bless you, Daddy,
do not forget me in your prayers.

The Brave Day

The day is a brave soldier.
I sleep during the light, and do
not know what goes on. The age
of worldwide communication is
not for me. I was made for a
sheltered existence.

The Shaded Life

I was made for a quiet life
on the plains. My attraction to
the city is eager and joyful and
fervent, but my strength is only
as resilient as the lace hanging
at my meadow-windows.

Motherhood

Mayn't I be a mother?
Mayn't I shelter a young thing
with my nurturing wing? Mayn't
I shower an infant with kisses and
cuddles? Give a baby a bath? Walk
a toddler in the grass? Pick flowers
with a bright child? Teach a young
woman to read, or a young man to
grow. Mayn't I love one uncondi-
tionally? Mayn't I be a mother?

Boyfriend Qualities I Admire

Humble mind,
Sincerely kind,
Nightly love,
Morning dove.

Imagining I Were A Bug

The ceiling crashes down upon me.

I struggle beneath the weight like a small bug.
The ceiling is very heavy, and it squashes me.
I scream, but nobody hears my scream.

Eyre, Eyre

Jane was a character of strength,
enduring wit, humor, and grace. Her
story uplifts me, and reassures me. It is
like watching my favorite ballerina dance.

In the Raining Forest

This world was built by God,
and given to us. Framed in gold
and hung on the placid blue wall in
the raining green forest, this world is.

Beautiful Thoughts

I've seen beauty like this before.
I've known happiness like this before.

It feels just as I remember it. Lord, my
body reeks; but my thoughts
are of lily of the valley.

Cry With Me

Wherefore dost thou cry?
Hunger and bliss come and go.
Since I have never understood this
life, I will cry too. Cry with me.

My Hands

My hands are long-fingered and
short-focused. They know what they do.
They work calmly and intelligently. My hands
are blessed with strength, grace, and capacity.
The Lord has blessed me with these hands.

Do Not Turn Away From Me

I would like to be part of a family
that endures. Daily I come calmly and
peacefully to thee, as a deer to water.
Please do not turn away from me.

I Have All The Colors

I have a desire to please,
and a great love for the unwanted.
I have all the things the Lord gave to me.
I have legs, hands, eyes, mouth, shoulders,
ankles, thoughts, dreams, prizes, failures.
I have all the colors of the rainbow in
my bosom, in my grand body.

For My Coworker

God bless the people I see each day.
The sacrifices they give are worth more
than the money paid me by the corporation
for which I work.

Friend

Her dressing is haphazard, and her
hair is a mess, but her voice is
beautiful and her face pure.

Imaginary Piety

Piety, what dost thou look like? I've known
nothing so lovely as thee, imaginatively.

Woman, I Remember You

Woman, I remember your face, your
straightforward way of speaking, your laughter,
your cigarettes, your vulgar jokes, your sweetness,
your crassness, your child, your sister, your mother,
your home. Woman, I remember you.

The Brain Needs Fat

One cannot live well if one has not dined well,
wrote Virginia Woolf. To live is to think and work
and create and love and move and dance. Do not give
up these things for the sake of being thin. Fat fuels the
brain. Everything of the body requires nourishment.

Natural Way of Being

My natural way of being is different than
the preferred way of being. I struggle thus
and enjoy thus. My life unfolds before me,
by the patience and planning of the Lord.

Consumed

The computer screen consumes me.
The digital world calls to me. My Mind
is capable of no philosophy / poetry whilst
I gaze into the blue, electronic space.

Failing At Love

The relationships of humans make for good
entertainment. Human love is ruined by worldly
hungers. We are troubled because we cannot satisfy
one another. I fail often enough!

I Am Desperately Human

My laziness and impatience
are excessively enough.

Prayer for My Brethren

May you love thy soul more than thy
life, for only then will you know peace.

When I write to you, my brethren, mere
words can only somewhat express what I
wish to convey to you.

Thy Passions Are Battling Within Thee

May the language of the Lord's heart
speak to thee & help thee to overcome
thy treacherous passions.

Forever

To sincerely love one's soul
more than one's life is to empathize
with the creator of all things, for souls
last forever, and so shall our Creator.

Work Uniform

My blue shirt labels my loyalty,
proclaims my patronage, calls out
my duty, betrays my apathetic role
in the professional world.

Dreaming for Gifts

Of all the gifts I wish to receive,
I want motherhood the most. I dream
of holding bald babies against my bosom.

Come

Come hither, boy.
I've dreamt of you;
Come near to me.

Honestly and Faithfully

People keep us truthful if we let them—
if we do not shut them out, they will help us
to live Honestly and Faithfully in community.
Family and friends assist in opening our hearts
and minds. We will edify ourselves only when
we extend human compassion to one another.

The Public Ways of Men

Men have an energy and intelligence that I do not possess.
I accept my understood femininity and I accept their foreign
masculinity. I accept our differences. I accept the public ways
of men, and the private way of women.

My Eating Disorder Educates Me

The Lord will shine upon me;
my eating disorder tells me so.
Why else would I have suffered,
but for ultimate clarity & purpose?

Uplifting Efforts

Overeaters Anonymous, your efforts
and existence are uplifting, wonderful,
and good. I've left your rooms but not
your beliefs and proverbs. One day at
a time. Easy does it. Step by step.

For My Roommate

For my friend, who gives me hope;
I shall give him anything in return.

Holy Hunger

Always have I struggled with a great hunger
for fulfillment. The world is not enough. I want.
The vacuity of my mind, heart and inner being is
tremendous. So, I eat. Now, my stomach is filled
to the brim and my heart is left out in the cold.
I guess I was hungry for God and not food.

Contentment is a Choice

Contentment is a conscious choice,
a monumental matter of the will.

I Do Not Eat Unplanned Meals

This body I was given to inhabit appreciates
routine meals and daily nutritional normalcy.

The Heart of a Dancer

Ballet finishes me. I have
a ballet-sized hole in my heart.

The Lord Came To Me

The Lord came to me and spoke thus:
Child, I give you the gift of dance to soothe
your troubled mind and frustrated body. Its grace
will comfort you. Its technique will free you. As a
sign of my love for you, I give you Dance.

To Complain Tragically

There are always things about which to complain
tragically, dramatically, murderously. I shall shut
my mouth to all complaining, for it takes away; it
lessens the beautiful miracle of life.

I Pray For Things of My Understanding

I pray for the things of my understanding. I cannot
pray for those things I do not understand. In his letter,
he said that he was full of hope. I shall pray for hope.

For Jay, My Friend

I pray that God will bless thee beyond
thy wildest dreams. I've watched you
live ruthlessly, artistically, painfully.
Jesus loves thee more than human
words are capable of explaining.
Drink it all in. I believe that thy
gifts and abilities were given thee
by Our Lord, ruler of the universe. I
believe that God is so in love with you
that no other lovely creation can compare.
For a love of His size there is no substitute.

Roundabout Motion of Love

Beginnings and endings, circles and squares,
wherefore dost thou goest? Take me there!

I hold his beloved face in my mind wherever
I traverse. I hold it gingerly lest it evaporate!

I am mother and sister and girlfriend and wife,
neice, grandmother, and friend. I am to thee, all
things earthly and human!

Seek God for spiritual fulfillment. Ask God for
what I cannot give. Hunger well for the Lord!

Life with the Lord

My body is not mine. My human thoughts and actions
are not mine. I exist beyond this world. I live in another
realm. My beliefs and morals are not my own. I belong
sincerely to the Lord. I long calmly and mightily for
the Lord. I hunger for no human food. I breathe
only out of habit. I obey my spirit humbly,
but elsewhere, in the arms of the Lord.

In Loyalty and Liberty

In loyalty and liberty,
I live and work. My mind is
watchful and prudent. Mine hands
are capable and strong. Mine legs are
 swift & brave. God Bless America,
carnal country that I love!

Steps for a Good Life

Unto Him I struggle.
Unto Him I pray.
Unto Him I submit.
Unto Him I come.

Bulimia Woos Me

Bulimia woos me and lures me like no
man or woman has before. The temptation
to sin is very great. By resisting my passion
I will find peace. Succumbing to passion is
not the path to peace. How can it be, when
bingeing is an avalanche in my mouth &
throwing up a volcano in my brain?

What is Christmas

Winter beauty, stable cheer, the
Lord came down, my life is here!

Overeating

Instability, apathy, gluttony, paranoia.
I shall die my death, plunged in a bowl
of potatoes. Jesus, fix me. I am a ruthless
sinner, hungry for more, but dying of emp-
tiness. How can it be, this dichotomy?

Nice Things He Said To Me

I know that you do not want to use more gas,
but there's gotta be somewhere we can go. *And,*
loving you was never a burden, it was a pleasure.

I Am Unable to Live Perfectly

I am unable to unite the lives and dreams
of my ancestors. Many beautiful people, and
one unbeautiful descendant.

If I Were A Frog

I'd like to be a frog, unknown
and anonymous, like lovely Emily
Dickinson. Or was she a toad?

The Hunger In Me Clashes With My Pride

The hunger in me clashes with the pride in me.
I am drawn downward by my hunger and upward
by my pride. The love in me clashes with the apathy
in me. I am drawn outward by my love and inward
by my apathy.

Those Who Look To Jesus, Look To Truth

Those who look to Jesus, look to truth,
and life stretches out wide before them.

My Body and Soul Remember

How can I ever repay him for loving me? As closely as
I understand Jesus, I understand him. There is no wealth or
success that I should adore in him. There is no beauty or glory
that I should desire in him. All that I know about holiness I have
learned from him: body of the bark of a tree, soul of a spring of
water, eyes of earth, and hands of sky. Yes, my body and soul
remember.

Submission

Submission is my name. I do not require praise or power.
Submission is my name. I write humble poetry and beg for
forgiveness. Submission is my name. I give myself to you.

Feelings of Inadequacy

Feelings of inadequacy and hunger and hurt whelm me
over and under and through and in and out and always.

Things That Impress Me

The ability to dance, to sing, to draw, to write, to
sincerely love. The fathomless depth of the devotion
of our Lord. My own rudeness. My raw, restless mind.

Marilyn Monroe

I obey the gods that tell me to strive for beauty.
So demure, so angelic, so sweet and blond was she!
I wish to be more like thy image, Miss Monroe, and
less like me!

I Look To You For Answers

"I look to you for answers," she said to me, this small pixie
of a girl, this wise bear of a woman. Why does she look to me?
I've done nothing to warrant her respect, her interest, her love.
Her intelligence and wit far exceed my own.

Composite Human Being

Every moment of my life embellishes my person. If I do
not consciously remember each moment, then my soul—
which is enmeshed with my body—remembers.

The Rain Washes the Town

The rain washes the town, the pavement, the cars,
the banks, the stores. When I exit this building, I too
will be washed.

The Decision to Pray

I believe in God, though I fight with comfort, sanity, and
sexuality. I struggle fully and completely. I admit my own
abilities and flaws. I've come knowingly to the end of
my rope. I will pray, I will pray, I will pray!

Though Innocent

Though innocent in his disease, he is guilty in his sin. I know
that you love him more than he can comprehend. Only you can
bless his life, change his heart, and complete his vision. I believe
in you, Lord.

Lavish Your Heavenly Love

Dear God, lavish your love upon the men
I've loved. Thank you for sending your son,
and for making me clean.

Dear Woeful God

Dear God, help me to know my
true self. Put me in touch with the
woman inside the heart of me. I've
cried silently and plentifully.

The Woman and Groom

The woman and groom died calmly in the arms of one another.
They could not live together, and they could not live alone. They
could not live in this world, nor could they be in any other. Where
snails and worms roam; that is where they wanted to go. So they
huddled closely together for warmth, and traveled to a place
far outside the pages of our book.

The Presents Overflow

Too much money spent! My heart feels greedy. Christmas purely
created, is a misguided circus. *Noel* is both French and English for
'a joyful shout expressing exhilaration for the birth of Christ.' But
where is the birthchild? Hidden under all the presents?

What Comes Slowly Surely Comes

What comes slowly surely comes. My patience is tried
and true. My love will return to me, when he is ready. His
hands will read me like Braille. My body is a book, written
by our Lord. I shall open and turn the pages for My love.

Winter Prayer

Winter beauty, prince of snow,
king of my heart always. Lavish
your love on Jay, Lord! Give him
my portion, as well!

Come to Me, Art and Beauty

Come to me art, beauty, grace, handmade
and homemade, god-given, earth-embraced,

love-lavished, peace-provided, come to me,
Christmas festivities and celebration!

If People Were Made of Light

If people were made of light, and light of
energy, and energy of everything, then I and
you are similar to stars. We match in lumination
and radiance. Let us shine!

Lord, I Need To Hear You

Lord, may I hear you? I need to hear you.
My life depends on it. I need you. Bless my
efforts, my tryings, my wants, my aches, my
gifts, my nothings. Thank you for not killing
me though I binged last night. Your commit-
ment to myself is hard to believe. I hope that
you will always love me. Lord Jesus, I truly
hope that you are real. Heal my legs. I am
sorry that I hurt them repeatedly. God,
heal my legs. Help me to believe.

The Contentment of Jesus

Discontentment brews bitterness brews pain brews frustration.
Teach me to be wise, untouched, and content in this world.

Shiningbrightness

If Einstein was right, then all matter is the same. People are made
of the same stuff as light. My hands are composed of stars, and my
hair of sunshine. I shall learn to bask in my own shiningbrightness.

The Weary World Rejoices

The weary world rejoices. Jesus came
to earth as God in flesh. A little bundle of
holiness; poor that we might be rich; forsaken
that we might be forgiven. (My weariness is a
product of worldliness and not of Him.)

Woman's Poem for a Man

How shall I please him?
My hesitancy and inadequacy
control my yearnings, my feelings,
my thoughts, my desires, my actions.
How can I please him? My womanli-
ness is nothing but dust and ashes.

Dear God, I Accept Your Sentence

Dear God, I accept your sentence,
your label on my brow, my breast.
You've made me pure. Thank you.

Prayer for Jeremy

Lavish your love upon Jeremy. Help him to
be steadfast in his projects, artwork, and ambition.
Help Jeremy to use the people around him as support,
sound boards, sweethearts, friends, unconditional accep-
tors and lovers. Help Jeremy to know that the mighty God
of the universe loves him completely, with purity & vastness.
Amen.

Bless Zola's Grandmother

Bless Zola's grandmother. Lay
your comforting hands upon her.
Let your abiding Love and Light
heal and soothe her aging body,
working mind, and full heart.

My Creed

Let all poetry be prayer, and all prayer poetry.

If I Should Pray For Thee

If I should only pray for thee,
and never see thee, then I would be
blessed with Love. I accept what is given
me by fate. I accept whole bodily and whole
soully all that I receive. The fruits of my life
are not sweet because they are dowsed in
sugar, but because they are the Lord's.

To Let Go of An Addiction

In order to let go of overeating, overpicking,
oversleeping and/or overanalyzing, focus on the
higher self; attend to the higher self. Everybody
has a higher self. The flesh profits nothing!

I Believe In A Savior

I will pray for my friend who says he "doesn't care."
This he voiced to me non-chalantly, haphazardly—and

I understood. I believe that he does care, so much that
 it hurts him and he tries to turn it off. Though, it is never
turned off; the caring continues. I believe that Jesus loves
my friend and I as much as any non-addicted persons. We
have a great potential for holiness. We are capable of
doing good. Holy trinity, show us the way.

Martyr for Art

Always, the vision of my thoughts knocks me off my
feet. My hungry heart tumbles out my chest by way of
thirsty hands. Blood pours holily out my mind, onto the
patient pages. I scream lavishly, hoping that somebody
will read; I pray that my mournful poetry will one day
prove my artistry!

Our Likenesses

My feelings for him are exquisite and relentless.
I understand his whims and moods. I understand his
desire to escape. I understand his love for art, poetry
and music. I too struggle with substance abuse and
an overpowering want for beauty.

Rob

I pray that you will hold Rob in your strong
hands every day of his life, though he does not
believe. May the Love and Grace I have for Rob
help to compensate for his lack of prayer. Open
Rob's beautiful heart, and lavish your lordly
love upon him!

The Body Does Not Know True Hunger

I have struggled in beauty,
in prayer, in true repentance.
I have struggled in thirst and
hunger, wildness and desire.

My body wants for food I
cannot possibly provide.

My soul's only wish is to
know comfort and peace.

What is to be my fate? Eating
is an endless job, a tireless hunt.

Balance of intake and output was
lost long ago. I cannot depend on
the body for it knows only one
request: More.

The Mind of My Soul

The mind of my soul rarely knows
or understands the mind of my body.

I cannot understand the ways of flesh,
or of temporal existence.

May the great struggle of my life cease
as I surrender to the mighty God of the
universe.

The mind of my soul is similar to
geese flying to the warm heart
of the Lord in winter.

Becoming Complete

If I should ignore the femininity & hunger inside
of me I might be calm. Help me, Jesus, to do so.

Shall Thereafter Die

If I open to the Lord my heart and my life,
then he will decide for me my path, my style,
my personality, my behaviors.

Instead, I am figuring out the perpetual stumble
on my own, doubtfully and prudently.

Oh, how prudent I am! God, give me a mind of
clarity and cleanliness, of fulfillment and joy.

I shall thereafter die peacefully, for I will
have lived peacefully and sensibly.

Jay's Hands

His hands tell me that I am real. His
hands tell me that I am attractive, wanted,
loved. I ache for his affirmation again and
again. I heap my burden upon him and he
never buckles beneath the weight. If it
were not for his deep, dark, obvious
humanness, I would think him a
god or angel of Perfection &
Sweet Immortality.

Never Enough Food

Upon eating my food, I want more.
Upon eating more, I want more. My ignoble

stomach gleefully accepts the overabundance of
fuel given it. I shall never have enough, for food
and love and drink tempt me all the same. I am
famished for all three. May the LORD bring
spiritual satisfaction to me so that I may
spiritually give to those around me.
Carnal fulfillment is meager,
but spiritual fulfillment is substantial
and good. Feed me Lord, as only you can.

What I've Done

I make love to my food,
as one who lives normally
would make love to a person.
I lavish touch, attention and joy
upon the plate, the pasta, the olive
oil, the seasoning. I wish for sobriety,
but what actions do I take to achieve it?
I pray for change, but to whom do I pray?

To What God Do I Give My Life?

I wish to turn myself in like a criminal who
knowingly and shamefully commits crime after
crime. I wish to give myself to the authorities, who
can care for me as they wish, as the good Lord governs
them. May my body be used for something good, and my
soul, too. I do not have need for them now.

I Shall Donate My Organs

I shall donate my brain to one comatose,
my legs to one immobile, my arms to one
helpless, my eyes to one blind, my ears to

one deaf, my saved soul to one desperate,
my spirit to one sad. I shall give all the
parts that I do not need to humanity,
to art, to science, to love.

To What Do I Owe My Life

To what do I pray, commit, devote daily? To what
do I dedicate, love, promise? God, where are you?

Unicorn

Motherhood is the unicorn I chase.
If blessed with the responsibility to
nurture a child, to unfold a person,
I will have arrived at my place in
life.

This World Makes Little Sense

This world makes little sense. So
much paperwork! I believe in words,
but I do not believe in paper or laws or
copies or offices or legality. The burdens
of this life feel like a truckload of rubbish
in my home, in my heart.

Barren People

Relief must be given to others,
in the form of love, luxurious love;
to those in our company, in our midst.
I do not understand the minds of others—
as I have said—but I do understand their
hearts. We all hunger the same.

Mired in Health

The lushness of my life
creates me ignorant to the pain
of others. I am beyond fortunate.
I am so comfortable that I balk at
disease. Teach me to be compass-
ionate, Lord.

Dear God, Speak Truth to My Heart

I desire no other words, no other voice,
than the voice of Thee. I shall study the
good book nightly. I shall pray daily.

Struggling for Nothing

I struggle to do well, but no good comes save from
you alone. My human efforts are worthless; I realize that
now. My trials and challenges stand for nothing. My pain and
heartaches hold no power, no influence. My self-deprecating ways
are sincere because thy face is the only face worth seeing. Thy soul
is the only soul worth knowing. My own soul is cruel and dishonest,
compared to thee. I struggle without merit. Forgive me, Lord.

Gifts For Thee

What can I give you, Lord? Thou hast
everything. The whole world belongs to
thee. I shall work and labor for thee. My
sweat and tears shall be thine. My body
shall belong to thee. My soul to thee,
as well. I seek only what you've
taught me to seek: truth and
goodness.

Love in the Past

I've loved you in the past,
but what am I worth? I am
unpredictable and weak and
fragile: a single blade of grass
trampled beneath the mud. I am
one mere person.

An Artist's Prayer

Use me, Lord. Use me fully and completely
for thine own pleasure! My hands are yours.

Capability Expanded

His personality and style inspire purity.
They enlarge my purity. He increases my
knowledge of people, my love for people. He
shows me with his sincere eyes how to care, how
to be holy in the treatment of others. He accepts my
faults & the faults of others. Though indiscretions do
not please him, he realizes that they do occur and will
continue to occur. He knows that he is not God, that his
opinions matter only slightly. He expresses his love. He
will not judge me, but will humor me with his laughter
and acceptance of me. I grow in my pastor's presence.

My heart happily recognizes this compassion, this
mercy in human form. Perhaps the definition of
inspiration is *to expand one's desire to love.*

My Pastor

My pastor presents a kind man to the world.
He gives what Jesus would want him to give.

He honors the lives of others. He teaches with his
words, his eyes, and his treatment of us. We under-
stand humility because of him.

Walls Surrounding My Heart

Darling life, I wonder why you continue for me,
so gallantly, so nobly. I do not believe in my own
strength or capability. I do not excel at anything in
particular. My attempts are unworthy. I am a mass
of confusion, effort, and error. I am deaf to many
things: to sadness, to compassion, to sin. I am
handicapped to clarity, to love. Because of
my admission of these things, Lord, will
you change me, empower me, save
me from myself?

My Love of the Truth is Preposterous

My love of the truth confounds me. How can
I so desperately yearn for all that is true but also
feel nothing save disappointment, hurt, shame. My
heart may try to open briefly, swiftly, nonchalantly,
but then the wind gently closes it!, and the truth I so
beautifully love is out of reach again.

Then, I Will Be Kind

I've always wanted to be kind.
Later, I thought, later I will be kind,
when I am no longer hungry; when I am
filled, when I am satisfied. Then, THEN I
will be kind.

Loving Others is Exhausting

Loving others is exhausting.
Are you as weak as I am,
dear friend, are you?

I Would Like to Be Holy

I would like to be holy. My incessant eating
holds me back. May my stomach be not my god.
May only my God be my god. Infiltrate my body,
Lord. Fill my soul with thee so that I may live. For
food steals my peace daily. I need your grace more
than anything else. I would like to be holy, Lord.

I Am Thankful, Lord

I am thankful, Lord, to have a job
that supports me and holds me
earthily, as you do holily.

He Calls Me

He calls me on the phone, but there
is nothing to talk about. We struggle for
words. Why is there nothing to say to one
another; nothing of interest or value? Still,
I love him; my heart yearns for him. <3

If Everything I Did Were Literal

If everything I did were literal, then my heart would be
in a million pieces each morning when I wake to the world;

tiny pieces on the bedroom floor, spilled out from under the
white sheets of my poet's bed. I am broken by the beauty of
the world nightly. Jesus, piece me together daily.

The Wisdom of A Kempis

"Put aside earthly wisdom, and all
seeking to please the world and thyself."
The wisdom of Thomas A Kempis pierces
an arrow through my heart.

We All Desire to Satisfy Ourselves

We all desire to satisfy ourselves. The people laden
with themselves are burdened more than the others. I'm
hungry for splendor but ignorant of how to get it; hungry
for my own needs to be met, but ignorant of the needs of
others. I sit stoically, delightfully, innocently, in my place
at the McDonalds, writing about others, who are
actually just like me.

How May I Best Serve Others?

Dear God, how may I best serve others?
Lovely Lord, allow me to write exquisite poetry
for thee. Beauty shall ooze out my fingertips. I shall
belong to you, because I am sincere, because I am of
the lowborn, because I desire nothing for my own glory,
and everything for thine glory, my lovely Lord.

Letter from Above

I hope you dance, Melanie. I hope
your heart is heavy with knowledge,

and at the same time light with My
Love. Be happy and be free!

My Job, As I See It

I have been commissioned
by the Lord to provide poetry and
dancing (are they not the same?) for
others; to provide the opportunity for
poetry and dancing for others.

This means always paying my way and not
causing others to stumble.

This means writing extensively; and with great love.

This means conducting business honestly and humbly.

This means dressing simply and treating others sweetly.

This means demanding no special attention or treatment.

This means travelling freely between Pennsylvania and
New York.

This means giving framed photographs and cards to
family and friends.

This means embodying peace and poetry and com-
passion to the best of my ability.

This means accepting the employment life gives
and making do.

This means living comfortably with little.

This means maintaining an open mind
and heart.

Lord, help me! I need help to do
my job well.

Personal Pride

Personal pride avails me no thing.
I falter as a flower would in the rain,
beneath my human pride.

Individuality

Everybody seeks individuality. I
hunger as a vampire would for blood:
to be rare and treasured, to be captivating.
My hands race against time, trying to create
extraordinary things, precious things, wonder-
ful things—but only God can do that.

Words for the Downtrodden

Ridiculed, derided, and mocked
by the people, I am complete in Christ.
Offended, rejected, and weakened by those
who share my design and makeup, I can do all
things through Christ who strengthens me. Poor,
depleted and run dry by humans, I am rich in
Christ.

Lies Are Not Honest

Lies are not honesty. Do not trust your own
lies. Living in the city, yearning for air; living in
the country, yearning for suffocation. Completely
confused about where to live, I am confident in
Christ. Christ is my king and my number one
ally. I can live neither alone nor with others
without Him.

I Am A Flow of Food

I am not a body. I am a flow of food.

The Natural Look

Don't do anything to your nails or your hair,
he said to me, I like the natural look. Sometimes
appeasing others is appeasing the self; serving the
Lord is serving nature and simplicity. I delight in
the agreement of God, myself and others!

Eve and Matthew

Eve and Matthew have a child named Ophelia. I
smile at their standard family, their house of organic
fabrics and natural foods. I imagine baking bread and
soap smells emanating from baby, mother, and father,
in a place where style is only functional and beauty
overrated. Let me live your life, but let me not
worship manmade health standards.

Who Will Keep Me Safe

Who will keep me safe,
Lord, when the thunder
quakes my house?

Dream Attacker

Last night, I dreamt a man was chasing me with a knife,
wanting to cut my fingers off. My fear was heightened by

the familiarity of the attacker. I felt that he was everywhere and that I could not get away from him. My fear of life overwhelms me. If only God would keep me safe, in my dreams and in my waking, as he promised he would.

Do Not Kiss Me

He tried to kiss me at the end of
the night and of course I pulled away,
not because I am afraid, or playing hard
to get, but because my soul knows what
it wants, and it does not want him.

Purely His

I am not attracted to him sexually
or romantically. My love for this person
is perfect and spiritual. I have only a spiritual
desire to know him. I have only an artistic ethos
to desire him. I have no feelings of partnership or
mateship for him. He knows this. Why does he
test me?

Conundrum

I aspire to let everything I do reflect my love
for the great, gentle Truth. I aspire to live simply
and walk humbly. I aspire to dance and create and
express my fallen self as sincerely as possible, for
my sincerity is the Lord's and so is my passion.

I Ride My Own Melt

My person, my precious person,
is a being of the Lord, stamped by

the Lord, known by the Lord, branded
and numbered by the Lord, chained by
the Lord: no acting and no pretense.

Evolution

We have in many ways evolved, but subtley.
We have extravagantly devolved. Disease and
obesity ravage us. (I am one victim.) Our Christ-
like perfection-seeking is vastly troubled. I worry
for the future, Lord. I am choked by worry. These
rhymes and words reflect my worry.

I Cannot Believe in Myself

Directly my appearance
reflects my thoughts. I am
a person on hold, numb and
stunned by disbelief in myself,
in humanity, in all that I care for.

Bless My Friends

Dear Lord, bless my friends Julie and Justin, poets and artists
in every cell of their beings. Bless Zola's grandmother, help her
to live well, to use her energies well. Bless my mother, Mary, to
be not anxious, be not tense. Bless my father, whose heart and
mind are intelligent and quiet. Bless my brother Adam, who
fearlessly and energetically prevails. Bless my sister Julie,
whose courage and sacrifice are stunning. Bless Gail in
her strength and independence. Bless Kathryn in her
creativity and beauty. Bless the hearts of those I
love and of those I do not love. Bless all the
noble children, my Lord.

Offering

Take Jay. Take his body and do with it thy perfect will.
Take my body and create something good of it. I have no
more ideas, no more inspiration. I am out of love and joy.
I am used up, My Lord. Take me. Take us. I hand BOTH
of us over to thee. Have compassion on us, Mighty God!

Forgive Me, Lord

Forgive me, Lord, I know not what I do.
I know nothing, even. I am caused detrimental
sadness by the shunning of my friends. And, why?
Am I not fully satisfied in Thee? Am I not overjoyed
in Thy presence alone? Am I not fully provided for and
completely loved by Thee? Am I not Yours alone?

What Do They Think Of Me

Do they think I do not feel? Do they think,
that because I call myself an artist, a creative
person, that sentimentality and emotion mean
nothing to me? I feel, my Lord. I hurt. I have
pain like the others. But you know this. You
know everything about me. I have nothing
new to say, my Lord.

The Simplicity of My Soul

The simplicity of my soul complicates
my life, because I cannot uniform who I am
to the rest of them. They struggle to be rich and
I struggle to be poor. They struggle to be beautiful

and I struggle to be homely. They struggle to succeed
and I struggle to fail. They struggle to be pragmatic
and I struggle to be artistic. Who are we?

On His Birthday

If I cannot see him on his birthday with my
eyes, Lord, let me see him with my heart. Let me
see him with my understanding, my compassion, my
grace. Let me see him with my inner eye, round and
clear and holy.

The Desires of My Heart

God, bless the desires of my heart, the hungers
of my stomach, the confusions of my mind. Help me,
creator of the universe! Come into my heart and eat me
alive so that I may be food for Thee. I am completely
possessed by my eating disorder, but I would rather
be possessed by Thee. Love me as only you can.

What Troubles Me

What troubles me, my Lord? What burdens me?
What causes me such sickness of self, of body, of mind?
Let go all and thou shalt find all, they say. Surrender all &
thou shalt gain all. Must I surrender my poetry, my writing,
my art? Help me to give up what I hold dearest, Lord, if
it is not you.

Surrounded by Loved Ones

Surrounded by loved ones, I humbly receive their love and
affection. I happily acknowledge their comfort, companion-

ship, and comradery. Their words and kindnesses are precious to me. But why do I feel like I'm drowning in their love?

Valentine's Day

Come over to my heart, love. Valentine's
Day is here again and my lack of knowing
another intimately troubles me. But Your
grace is sufficient for me. I am Yours,
loving Lord! I shall wait patiently.

I Seek Everything I Ought Not To Seek For

I seek everything I ought not to seek; I desire every-
thing I ought not to desire; I thirst for everything I ought
not to thirst; I hunger for everything I ought not to hunger.
Where can truth and redemption be found?

*The first thirty years of my life have taught me that success
does not lie in New York City, or Los Angeles, or dancing, or
poetry, or pictures, or the affections of my peers, or money; but
rather, in the steady beating of my heart, and its ability to hear
God's gentle, persistent voice.*

By the grace of God, I am here today.
My life unravels before me and I watch the
colors and shapes pass by; they are beautiful,

Melanie M. Eyth

danceofmyhands@aol.com

42747714R00033

Made in the USA
Middletown, DE
20 April 2017